Koalas

Kate Riggs

seedlings

Published by Creative Paperbacks
P.O. Box 227, Mankato, Minnesota 56002
Creative Paperbacks is an imprint of
The Creative Company
www.thecreativecompany.us

Design and production by Ellen Huber
Art direction by Rita Marshall
Printed in the United States of America

Photographs by Can Stock Photo (James63), Getty Images
(Tim Graham, James Hager), iStockphoto (Peggy Chen,
Craig Dingle, Eric Isselée, Sawayasu Tsuji), Shutterstock
(Susan Flashman, Eric Isselee, worldswildlifewonders)

Library of Congress Cataloging-in-Publication Data
Riggs, Kate.
Koalas / Kate Riggs.
p. cm. — (Seedlings)
Includes bibliographical references and index.
Summary: A kindergarten-level introduction to koalas,
covering their growth process, behaviors, the trees they call
home, and such defining physical features as their clawed feet.
ISBN 978-1-60818-455-2 (hardcover)
ISBN 978-1-62832-044-2 (pbk)
1. Koala—Juvenile literature. I. Title.

QL737.M384R54 2014
599.2'5—dc23   2013029069

CCSS: RI.K.1, 2, 3, 4, 5, 6, 7;
RI.1.1, 2, 3, 4, 5, 6, 7; RF.K.1, 3; RF.1.1

First Edition
9 8 7 6 5 4 3 2 1

TABLE OF CONTENTS

Hello, koalas!

Koalas are animals
from Australia.
They live in trees.

Koalas are brown or gray. They have white fur on their chests, ears, and arms.

Koalas have claws on their feet.

Claws help
koalas go up trees.

Koalas eat eucalyptus (*yoo-kuh-LIP-tus*) leaves.

They eat bark and branches, too.

13

A baby koala is called a joey. The joey is born in its mother's pouch. Adult koalas live alone.

Koalas eat eucalyptus all day.

Then they get sleepy.

Goodbye,
koalas!

Picture a Koala

fur

nose

arm

leg

ear

eye

mouth

pouch

claw

Words to Know

claws: curved nails on the toes of
some animals

fur: the short, hairy coat of an animal

pouch: a pocket on the stomach of
a female koala

Read More

Galvin, Laura Gates. *Baby Koala and Mommy*.
Norwalk, Conn.: Soundprints, 2007.

Lang, Aubrey. *Baby Koala*.
Markham, Ontario: Fitzhenry & Whiteside, 2004.

Websites

Bellow Like a Koala
http://www.youtube.com/watch?v=0Z1M7BWFpwM
Learn how to sound like a male koala.

Enchanted Learning: Koalas
http://www.enchantedlearning.com/themes/koala.shtml
Print out pictures to color, and make a koala mask!

Index